WELCOMING LILITH

*Awakening and Welcoming
Pure Female Power*

Theresa C. Dintino

WELCOMING LILITH
Awakening and Welcoming Pure Female Power

ISBN: 978-1-944476-11-3

Library of Congress Control Number: 2013958119

Printed in the United States of America

Original cover art by Suzanne DeVeuve

For more on Theresa or her work, visit
http://www.thestregaandthedreamer.com
and
http://www.ritualgoddess.com

Dedication

To the Owl Goddess Lilith,
Welcome Back!

Contents

@

@

Introduction

I was living in rural Vermont when my 29th birthday arrived. Western astrology calls this the year of "The Saturn Return," the time life purpose is revealed. I returned from a party very late at night. Being rural Vermont, there were no streetlights. It was very dark. As I pulled into my driveway, my headlights illuminated a Great Gray Owl perched on the fence in my yard. Great Grays are rare in Vermont. It was very large and did not fly away.

Mesmerized, I emerged from the car slowly and quietly, and stood looking at the owl. Though I was quite close, the huge bird did not fly away. Our eyes locked in trance. The owl's eyes were huge yellow discs that I flew into; large, nocturnal suns that knew everything.

"What," I asked, for I felt an urgency, "have you come to tell me?"

"Save me from exile and banishment," the owl said.

What could that mean?

I did not understand, but knew the message must be important. The owl flew up into a tree. I continued to watch it by the light from my deck. It stayed on the branch looking down on me for a long time. That whole night I tossed and turned in bed. I knew this was some sort of visitation whose meaning I needed to decode. The owl would not let me sleep.

The next day I looked in all my books (this was before the Internet) for any information on owls and their symbolic meaning. I found that the owl is associated with hidden wisdom, secret teachings, and Lilith. Lilith? Who was Lilith? I had never heard of her. In my Webster's Dictionary, I found an entry for her: "Lilith, the first wife of Adam, before Eve."

What? Adam had a first wife?

I never knew that. I had been raised Catholic. Apparently, this part of the Lilith definition was from ancient Hebrew texts. The next day I took myself to the library and all local bookstores. I borrowed and bought every book I could find on Lilith, or that had a reference to her. There weren't that many. I found quite quickly that I was dealing with a banished Goddess and a forgotten reality of powerful ancient women.

Thus, the journey began.

At age 29 I was already identified as a writer. Now my lens shifted. I set out to write a nonfiction book about Lilith and these concurrent issues, but midway through, it flipped into two novels set in Bronze Age Crete about a Snake Priestess. Those are *Ode to Minoa* and *Stories They Told Me,* my Crete novels. The Owl Goddess, Lilith, appears in both of these novels as a character.

I continued to research and collect data on Lilith. The following is the result of the effort I started 20 years ago. She is not an easy one to pin down. I believe she wants it that way. Her presence is vast, multilayered, and multidimensional. It is not to be diminished.

The exploration in this small book is separated by subject into the many guises Lilith manifests in our culture, as well as how she is held in our psyches and collective mythology. This is only a start, an entry place for those who wish to know her, to welcome her back, to save her from exile and banishment in the world and within yourself. Take this beginning ride, then fly with her to where she wishes to take you. It will be different for everyone.

A great fragmentation of the female psyche happened with the banishment of Lilith. Or, one could reverse that to say: The Lilith story represents a great fragmentation still found to this day in the female psyche, in spite of all our advances toward "liberation" and "equality."

Which came first, the story or the fragmentation? Who knows? This book hopes to encourage the restoration of wholeness back to the female psyche, as well as all things female in the cultural and mythological realms. Until we restore ourselves to wholeness, we will never experience what we currently call "liberation" and "equality."

Preface

The Story of Lilith and Adam and Eve
(As told by Theresa C. Dintino)

Once there was a man and a woman, born at the same time, in the same place, of the same materials. Their names were Adam and Lilith. They lived together peacefully for a long time.

After a time, Adam decided that he wanted to rule over Lilith, but Lilith refused to submit to Adam. Being of equal origin, she saw no reason why she should. They began to argue—something they had never done before. Adam persisted. He even began to insist that she lie beneath him during intercourse. When she said no, he tried to force her. Lilith would not tolerate this behavior. She left Adam.

Adam howled and raged so loudly that none of the animals in the shared environment could find peace. Finally, they approached Adam, inquiring about the howling. He reported to them that Lilith had abandoned him. Could they find her and bring her back?

The animals found Lilith swimming in the warm waters of the Red Sea. She explained to them that Adam had behaved in a manner unacceptable to her. They told her that Adam was lonely and his moaning was keeping the whole world awake. Would she please return to him? Lilith stated to them that unless he accepted her as his equal, she would not return. Adam refused her request.

For a time, Lilith felt pain and loneliness, but she soon got over Adam, especially after she heard that he had a new wife whom he was treating badly.

Adam found a woman named Eve whom he wooed with a story she found flattering about a male God who had created her just for him out of one of his ribs while he was sleeping. Since she was younger and less experienced than Adam, she believed him when he told her that she was less of a person than him.

In this, Adam found great power and satisfaction. He even got to liking that feeling and began to search around for other ways of acquiring it. Still, oftentimes, especially at night, he found himself longing for that Strongwoman Lilith. Although Lilith never returned, Adam knew that she could if she wanted to. He also knew that he had wronged her. Because of this, he began to fear her. Worried that she may actually someday decide to return, he began to spread lies about her.

Eve was bothered by a feeling of duality, right from the start—a sort of shadow lurking. Since Adam never admitted to his first marriage, she could never come to understand it. She dared not tell anyone for fear they may call her insane, but sometimes she swore she heard the voice of another woman speaking to her. She still didn't know what it was that could have possibly made her eat that apple…

Chapter One

Lilith is a "Hairy" Woman

In junior high, in the mid '70s, I was one of the last girls to begin the lifelong ritual of shaving her legs. I can still remember how intensely I dreaded the arrival of gym class because we had to wear shorts, thereby exposing to all present the hairiness of me.

My mother never talked to us of matters such as these. Shaving, among other "feminine hygiene" concerns, was not discussed openly in our home. There had also been the recent conversation between my parents—loud enough for all of us to hear—concerning the increased amount of razor blades being used. They made a cutting remark toward my older sister who had only recently begun shaving. The gist of the discussion implied that not only were they displeased that she had started shaving, but that it was, for them, an expensive undertaking.

As a girl, the last thing I wanted to do was cause a problem (thank goodness that has changed), let alone inflict further financial strain upon my already overburdened parents. I dared not shave.

I was not alone. There was one other girl in my gym class whose legs also possessed the dreaded fuzz. In my humiliation, I used her as an anchor for my mind to cling to, telling myself over and over again, *I'm not the only one*. We both belonged to the same Roman Catholic church. I remember wondering even then if this had something to do with our delayed entrance into the rites of womanhood.

I obsessed on her legs the entire duration of the class. It was a daily ritual to stare at her legs, to determine how visible the hair actually was; measuring how close she had to get to me for me to see the hair. Her hair was darker and more abundant than mine. I found the greatest solace in that fact.

One day during gym class, while we were all observing my sister *hairy beast* on the balance beam, I made a horrifying discovery. Her legs were clean-shaven. Since the last gym class, she had entered the *secret society of shavers*.

I wanted to disappear, to sink beneath the floorboards, turn into a speck of dust upon the mat, or at the very least, run away to the comfort of full-length pants. I was the last girl in my gym class with hair on her legs. The one—the only one!—who had not started shaving. I knew everyone was looking at me. I knew everyone knew. I tried to take my mind off it, but it was no use. The only things that existed were my two hairy legs, exposed—beacons—for the entire world to see.

The feelings I had about myself at that moment seem so odd and inappropriate when I consider them now. I still shave, reluctantly, and I must add, quite sloppily. It's hard to do something well when you really don't care about it. However, when I try to stop or just go way too long between shaves, those same odd and inappropriate feelings rise up in me, surprising me still. I feel dirty, stinky, and masculine.

Through the ages, Lilith, the first feminist of the Western world, has been associated with hairy legs. Like any person banished for deviation and then excluded, rumors and stories grew around Lilith. In the Jewish Midrashim and throughout the esoteric texts of the Kabbalah, as well as Middle Eastern and European myth and folklore, they flourished. Like most rumors that grow out of fear, they are intensely negative and progressively more horrific.

One of the themes that pervades these stories is the fact that Lilith is a hairy woman. The long black hair on her head possesses magical powers. Demons may collect in the long locks, and they could possibly ensnare you. This is obviously a Gorgon/Medusa-like Goddess.

There was even the belief that you could tell if a woman was Lilith in disguise by the amount of hair upon her legs. To determine whether the Queen of Sheba was Lilith in disguise, King Solomon had a glass floor built around his throne. Upon approaching it, the Queen of Sheba thought it to be water. Wishing to keep her skirt dry, she lifted it, thereby exposing her hairy, Lilith legs.[1]

The third definition for "hairy" given in the Webster's New World Dictionary is: *difficult, distressing, harrowing.* Goodness knows, Lilith is all of these. And yet, all women, everywhere, grow hair upon their legs. If all women, everywhere, grow hair upon their legs, then all women are Lilith in disguise. Every time we obediently shave our own legs, we banish the Lilith within us back to the depths of the sea. In shaving off our hair, are we cutting, hiding, or rejecting our own inner power? Are we "grooming" it to fit acceptable standards of female power?

And what of those feelings I get when I do not? Dirty? Dirty: unclean, unpure, not virgin-like. My "pure" girl body turning into that of a woman's made me feel dirty. Abundant hair growth, triggering the need to shave, is but an indication, a visible outward sign, of what is to come next, if it has not come already; the most offensive thing of all that a woman's body insists on doing in spite of all the revulsion and disgust—bleeding.

Lilith is a raw, instinctual, physical female. I think it is safe to say that these particular rumors are true. Being a woman of Mediterranean descent, you can be sure she has a lot of hair, all over her body.

In traditional and ancient cultures, hair has long been a symbol of power—inner power manifesting itself in outward form. Of course Lilith is hairy. Her power is unquestionable. Of course she is "distressing, harrowing." She refuses to give that power up.

Ritual
Honoring the "Hairy" Self

Is there something about you that is "hairy," literally or metaphorically? Is there a way your inner power manifests outwardly that makes others uncomfortable? Call this hairy part up into the visual space in front of you. Look at it. Feel where it lives in your body.

Can you embrace it and love it? Maybe you already do. Send it some deliberate care and love. Do you allow it to thrive? Can you? Sit with that image and feeling. How might your life be different if you could allow this hairy part of you to flourish?

With this hairy part of you in mind, create a talisman for yourself made of hair—your hair or the hair of an animal, perhaps even horsehair. If you have no hair available, use yarn. Create the talisman to represent and remind you to love and honor your hairy Lilith self. You can add beads and decorations of your choice. Carry it with you or hang it somewhere you will see it often.

It was my sister, the one who had only recently been publicly shamed by my parents for her entrance into the *secret society of shavers*, who finally, understanding my shame and humiliation, encouraged me to shave. I'll never forget the day. It was late spring and we were taking down the laundry. The weather was warm, yet I continued to wear pants and tights. "Go ahead. Just do it," she urged. "You have to. You don't want to wear pants the rest of your life."

She was right. I sure didn't. That night I took a razor to my legs. The next day I wore shorts to school.

For years, when I thought back upon that fateful day in gym class, I would slip into a fantasy about having a mother who encouraged me to shave at a younger age to spare me all that pain and humiliation. My fantasy has changed. Now it is the fantasy of a mother who encourages her daughter *not* to shave. In my new fantasy, the mother argues a wonderful case against taking a razor to those tender, twelve-year-old legs.

Chapter Two

Lilith is a Bleeding Woman

In Talmudic lore God banishes Lilith for disobeying Adam and she is sent to live out her life in the Red Sea. Anyone who looks at a map can quickly determine the reasons for associations between women and this particular body of water. It has the shape of a vulva. There is also the matter of the color: *Red Water.*

Women are intimately connected with blood—the flow of life, "the watery realm of creation."[2] Our minds may separate from it, but our bodies never can. Our bodies will live out this life whether we pay attention or not. Of course, Lilith lives within and is at ease in the waters of the Red Sea. Lilith is not split from her body. This is indeed her "home."

This part of the story also identifies Lilith as a parthenogenetic Goddess, one who reproduces life from herself alone. In *The Women's Encyclopedia of Myths and Secrets,* Barbara Walker makes the connection between the name Lilith, the word Lily, and the "Goddess Juno who conceived her savior-son Mars with her own magic Lily, without any male aid." Walker notes: "This myth reflected the early belief in the self-fertilizing power of the yoni (vulva) which the Lily symbolized and Juno personified."[3] Walker also states, "Lilith's red sea was another version of Kali Ma's Ocean of Blood, which gave birth to all things but needed periodic sacrificial replenishment."[4]

Women bleed every single month for a full week, for a large portion of their lives. Yet in Western Culture, this is easy—even for a woman—to forget. It is to be taken care of and dealt with out of the public eye. Most women consider it to be a nuisance.

Hair growing on certain parts of the female body heralds the completely overlooked crossing of the threshold from girlhood into womanhood. With the entrance into womanhood comes the monthly connection to her moon-tide, the rhythmic possibility of conception, followed by either fertilization or the death of that possibility. This *death of possibility,* which the body releases as "moontime blood," is one of the most cleansing and healing processes known. Lilith embraces her moontime blood. She swims in its depths. She creates of it and herself more life. This is the reality Lilith exists within. Yet, for so many years now on this planet, this cycle and process of cleansing have been considered unpure, disgusting, and dirty.

For all our science and study it is still completely unclear, from a scientific point of view, why human women bleed the way they do. But women know why. We know we bleed because blood carries the life force, and female bodies create and regenerate life.

Red. That most sacred and holy color to early people, signifying possibility and the creativity which arises from pure possibility. For a woman, this cycle of possibility occurs within her over and over again every single moon. The ancients recognized and honored not only the possibility of conception of an actual child, but this sacred cycle as a reference point for possibility in all areas of our lives. Always in Paleolithic and Neolithic times, the precious dead were buried with red ochre to reassure their return to life through the blood-filled womb of a female body.

If we would but free ourselves to remember the deep wisdom this actual *felt* experience has to offer us about the circular cycles of life and death, what leaps and bounds could be made in the realm of human consciousness.

Lilith is a woman of tremendous power who knows the source of her power—her wise blood—is generated by her own womb.

Ritual
Honoring Our Sacred Moontime Blood

Menstrual blood is the most sacred liquid on the planet. Until the modern era, women ritually returned their sacred blood to the Earth, knowing that this was a gift their bodies created that the Earth needed. Modern women giving their blood back to the Earth once again would have a profoundly healing effect upon the planet. If you are a woman who is still bleeding, take some time to collect all or some of your moontime blood and offer it, in sacred gesture, back to the Earth. She needs it. Do this in an honoring way, using rituals that feel right to you. Offer this precious red liquid to the trees, to the waters, to the soil, to the mountains, to the stones, in honor of ancestors, with prayers for protection. This is not only a precious gift and offering, it lets the trees, mountains, and waters know what is happening in the wombs of human women.

If you are a woman whose cycles of bleeding have ended, offer instead red liquid from plant materials on a monthly, or some sort of rhythmic basis, in accord with the moon. Do this in honor of all the blood your body created and all the creativity still flowing through you.

The only way back to true power is by reclaiming our true femaleness. We can start by recognizing and acknowledging the bodily experience that is uniquely female: our sacred moontime blood. We need to fall back in love with the flowing rivers of red water running within, between, and through us.

Chapter Three

Lilith is a Raging Woman

Let's talk about the madwoman; about Bertha Mason—the dark woman—running, wild and raging, through the attic of the home of the man Jane Eyre loves.

Let's talk about Rochester's first wife—abandoned, banished, and unaccepted, the same as Adam's first wife, Lilith. Let's talk about Eve and Jane Eyre and what we all know to be true: that woman in the attic, that snake in the tree, is only the shadow sister, a split-off part—the furious female.

More than any other book I had ever read, *Jane Eyre* captivated and moved something deep and ancient within me. The character of

Bertha Mason lingered, haunting me. Charlotte Brontë has been accused by many, including Virginia Woolf, of letting her anger show through in her writing.

The accusation in and of itself implies that letting one's anger show through in their art is somehow an inappropriate thing to do (for a woman, anyway). If art is an expression of the truth, on the deepest level, why aren't we surrounded by the art of furious women? Ours is a society that absolutely rejects angry women. Even when expressed, our anger is ignored, trivialized, and rejected. It is rarely acknowledged as something that must be dealt with—as a feeling expressing a need for action. Charlotte Brontë has been called "a raging woman." How I love her for that.

Women, in spite of all our accomplishments, have failed to deal with our anger. That anger, however, is the key that will open the door out of our present state of perpetual angst, for beneath that anger—on the other side of it—is a woman's power. The only way to the power is a path passing directly through the rage. That is the path women have refused to take.

What does it mean to be mad? Is the madwoman insane? Crazy with rage? To rage is to be mad. "Rage," Alice Miller says, "although an appropriate reaction to cruelty, is very often misinterpreted as the sign of innate mental imbalance."[5] The madwoman is not crazy. She is angry. She has been locked up for century upon century. She is abandoned, unaccepted, rejected, unacknowledged, unloved. She *feels* unlovable. Of course she is angry.

What does it mean to be angry? Anger is an emotion—a feeling. When experienced appropriately, it is a fleeting surge within us, a signal or warning the body sends to the psyche saying... *something is not right here.*

For women, anger is no longer a mood or a fleeting feeling. It has become a disembodied spirit, floating around separate from our physical and emotional selves. It has taken on a life of its own, become the horrified other. Anger is now our shadow sister, locked away in the attic or banished to the Red Sea—something we live in fear others may uncover, something of which we are truly ashamed.

Most women do not see themselves as angry. In fact, if you were to suggest they might be angry, they would probably vehemently deny it. Angry is not something women wish to be. It is unpleasant, unattractive, and disturbing to everyone in the room. Anger, because it is conveniently mistaken for insanity, can attract the wrong kind of attention. Somewhere in the back of all our minds is the haunting knowledge, the memory that the expression of our anger can lead us to the same fate as that of Bertha Mason.

The character of Bertha Mason haunts us, not because she is a horrifying monster, but because we recognize ourselves in her. Bertha leaves us with the eerie knowledge: *She is me. I am her.* She is the part of myself I must repress—hide away—to ensure my safety, lest I become her.

Ritual
Honoring the Voice of Our Wombs

When Lilith was sent away, she became feared and fearful, even to women. What parts of yourself have you sent away because they are fearful? Do you ask your girlfriend to hide her true feelings because they make you uncomfortable? Do you tell people to not *rock the boat?* Are you afraid of conflict and therefore do things that are passive-aggressive? Let's face it, Lilith is not a good girl. She is not out to make others feel comfortable. *Making waves* is her forte. And because of this, Lilith is also not depressed or repressed. Because of this, Lilith is empowered.

Our wombs are the voice of knowing within us. We need to honor and listen to them. What feelings of anger, or others that feel unlovely and unfeminine, have you locked up in your womb space, creating great congestion within your own body and energy field? We need to speak the voice of our womb space. There are ways to own our anger, to listen to it, and then take its directives without hurting others. It is time we do this, and allow each other to do it. We need to listen to the voice of our anger.

Take some paper. Paint it red. Allow your womb's voice to flow over it with a pen, paintbrushes, or crayons. Paint or write with wild abandon all your womb has been holding. Really feel that you are expressing the voice of your womb.

Sit and listen to all that has come forward. Honor it all with greetings. Take some white sage or some other kind of material to burn that creates cleansing and purifying smoke. Allow the smoke to flow over the paper, allow the smoke to flow around the area of your own second chakra. See these feelings, and any toxicities being cleaned, purified, and released.

Then, crunch up the paper and offer it to the Earth in a burial ritual, just as ancient women buried the placenta. Let the Earth hear this voice of your womb.

Chapter Four

Lilith is the Muse

In the philosophy of the four temperaments, a system used to diagnose the personality types through the Middle Ages and earlier, the planet Saturn rules the liquids of the spleen, the black bile. The person influenced by this planet is often described as "bitter, irritable—of melancholic disposition."[6] They are also, however, attributed with possessing "genius," frequently expressed in a creative outlet. Lilith is associated with Saturn.

Jungian scholar Siegmund Hurwitz describes what he calls a *creative melancholy* that many people of Saturnine nature experience before the onset of a creative endeavor. In the Saturnine depressions his clients often see a dark, winged woman who is interpreted to be

Lilith.

Several of the individuals Hurwitz uses as examples of people with a Saturnine nature reach the remarkable understanding within themselves that these "depressions" are intricately connected with their creative process. They perceive the melancholy as being the other side of their genius. They instinctively know that without the bouts of depression they would not be able to "create"—that the depression and the creativity spring from the selfsame well.

Astrologically, the planet Saturn is the planet of limitations, restrictions, discipline, and order. Saturn represents authority, the rules we live by. It is also thought of as the "wise teacher," the bearer of lessons—most specifically lessons that are repeated over and over until we finally, exhaustedly, learn them.

It seems to me that dealing with our anger is the collective Saturnine lesson for women now. It is we who must design more creative, less destructive ways of channeling our fury. This is our work. It is our work because it is our anger. It is we who are experiencing it.

It is quite commonly known that beneath the surface of depression lies rage—an anger repressed to such an extent that it has become truly frightening. If a person really wants to recover, heal herself, become undepressed—she must experience her rage. Anger, though not the only cause of depression or the sole emotion to be repressed, is most often the first encountered, right there on top, when the depressed person dips below the surface of their depression and begins to get into the muck of the *dis-ease*.

Depression is a going down, a lowering, an invitation to go yet deeper within. A time to "face our demons." We call those things that frighten us, but that we know are unconsciously motivating us, "demons."

It is Mary Daly who calls a woman's demon her genius; who reminds us of the original meaning of the word: *an attendant, ministering or indwelling power or spirit; Daimonion: Genius.*[7]

The inner demon is also the muse. In this way Lilith is truly demonic. Lilith is creative genius, born only in darkness. She must be recognized, accepted, brought back into the light. She is the powerful woman inside of us whom we continue to send away, reject, and abandon. It is she who is generating all the rage.

Because we perceive it as a black hole within us, a place from which, once entered, we shall never again emerge, we resist and refuse the journey. As women, we have not yet understood that there is indeed an end, something on the other side of that dark tunnel of rage—a life with power.

Where do we begin? We begin by ceasing to refer to ourselves as depressed. We begin by admitting finally to what is really going on inside of us. We must feel it, in every cell of our being, and then we must release it.[8]

Yes, the darkness will engulf us, the rage will temporarily swallow us. So begins the process of digestion. Only through digestion is one able to assimilate, integrate, and eventually, through release, set oneself free.

Ritual
Welcoming Lilith

If the dark, winged Goddess comes to you, will you send her away? What would you say to her if she came? Perhaps it is time to summon her to you. If she holds your creative potential, that may be a good thing to do.

What might she be holding for you? Read this ritual first. Take some time to sit with the idea of it. Hold this ritual in your consciousness. Decide where you want to do this. Then, when you are ready, prepare the space to carry it out, both internally and externally.

Close your eyes. Call the dark, winged Goddess to you. "Lilith, I am ready to receive you."

She may fly in. She may walk in. She may simply appear as woman, owl, or snake.

When she comes to you, she will be holding a gift. She will hand this gift to you. This is yours. She has been holding it for you. Can you see it? What will you do with this gift?

Chapter Five

Lilith is a Woman of Power

Power is the life force that wants to flow through us, make things happen, cause movement.

When I speak of a woman's power, I do not speak of the commonly held assumptions around the meaning of power: power over something else or brute physical force. When I speak of women's power, I speak of our magic, I speak of our intuition, I speak of our ability to synch ourselves with our ecosystem, to deeply listen to the womb of the Earth and the womb of the galaxy through our own womb space. I speak of our "inner ears" and synaesthetic senses, our power to give life, our power to feed life, our power to care for life. We are the life-givers. This offers us a special power and a special responsibility to the planet. Our power is nothing less than the power of the Goddess.

Once women danced. They danced in circles. They danced alone and together. They joined hands and spun, raising the cone of power. They held their arms—like antennae—above their heads, breasts forward, buttocks back, and moved. Their movement created energy. This energy grew within them, creating more energy, until it began to move through them, around them, between them, power increasing in the sharing of power.

All over the ancient world, women danced. Scattered through the art and remains of unearthed civilizations of the past are sculptures, paintings, and images of women dancing.

"Kundalini" is the term Hindus use to describe the energy that lies coiled, dormant, at the base of the spine until, through movement, one awakens it. It is also referred to as the *serpent of fire.*[9] It is our power and it comes from the inner Earth.

Depictions of snakes are preponderant in these ancient cultures, as well. Ancient women knew the serpent within them. They understood that movement—dance—could awaken that serpent, help it climb the pillar of their etheric spinal column and lead them to transcendence, enlightenment, and spiritual bliss. They called Her the Goddess.

True power starts in the Earth and moves up into the belly, up through the spine. It is energy in motion.

Modern women, afraid of our power, afraid of the consequences the invocation of our power may provoke, sensing danger even in the simple act of swinging our hips, decline Her invitation, ignore the desire we feel deep within us to move.

Ritual
Rekindling Your Own Power

Understand that power is relational. Sit with your vulva on the Earth, if possible with no clothing on. Feel that connection. Earth misses the connection with women's vulvas. See and feel the deep, dark center of the Earth. Call the Kundalini Goddess to you. See a liquid, gold-red energy coming up from that center through your vulva, into your womb space. Pull this delicious energy up through all your chakras with each breath, filling one at a time. Feel the Kundalini Goddess ignite your centers and empower your power. She is *lighting your fire*. Do this repeatedly, allowing the light to change colors as needed, until the serpent begins to dance inside you. Arise and embody the power by moving together and in harmony with Her. Feel this power in your body. Dance it. This is your power. Nurture it, live it, begin to embrace and embody it. Eventually, once there is enough energy, you may feel you want to share it.

Chapter Six

Lilith is a Black Woman

"Black is the color of creation. It is the womb out of which the new is born. It is also the color of night. Black is the maternal color and thus the black night gives birth to a new day."[10]

Black is the color of origin. It is the color of magic. Black is the color of power. The new moon, when the sun and the moon are in conjunction (on the same side of the Earth at the same time) renders the moon invisible. Yet they are both there, rising and setting together, making the pull on the Earth strongest in their shared direction. Lilith is associated with the new moon. She is a black woman, a Dark Goddess, a woman of color.

All the world over there have been found black female icons. They are referred to as "Black Madonnas" and "Dark Goddesses." They are consistently said to represent our darkness, that which we fear, the underworld, the so-called "negative" aspects of our personalities. The literature that is written about them echoes and repeats the word "chthonic." Chthonic means: dark, primitive, mysterious. This is not only a misinterpretation, but a misguided projection. Why must a black idol or icon be relegated to the realm of the chthonic?

If life originated in Africa, then the first human beings were black. That means the first woman was black; the first mother was black. If a deity is but a manifestation of divine power in a physical form, then it goes to follow that the first Goddess was black.

The first Goddess originated in Africa with the first humans. The first Priestesses fashioned a Goddess in their own likeness. This is not a chthonic symbol: it is the color of her skin. It is a black woman, a flesh and blood female, possessing the divine within her.

Seeing in the Dark

Early people were aware of the many ways in which their physical eyes could fool them. They were familiar with and accustomed to using senses beyond sight. They appreciated the meaning and absolute necessity of "inner vision," also called the "Eyes of the Goddess."

The Eyes of the Goddess was a prominent theme in the Paleolithic and Neolithic cultures of the Goddess. This gave them trust in what they could only perceive. In connecting with the Eyes of the Goddess, our ancestors were able to read messages in nature, acknowledge information from other realms, and access divinatory and oracular information. That which was unseen was accessible through the Eyes of the Goddess. They also had a deeply attuned ability to hearing what was not audible, understanding sound and no sound, decoding tone and frequency. They were able to listen to the voices in their heads, the clutching of their stomachs, decipher the "lumps" in their throats.

For most of human existence, the actual physical darkness was a time of interaction and communion with the other realms. Certain rituals were only performed in darkness. Within human darkness the stars could bring their light at these times; the deep cosmos could enter the hidden places in the psyche and offer *illumination*.

Circadian rhythms are extremely important for the biosphere of this planet. All are synched to this. Our bodies' inner glands use the darkness to produce hormones of darkness. Darkness and the dark times offer a different kind of growth than sunlight. Dark growth pulls from the deep underground well of the Earth. When the sun goes away, a different kind of food is produced and eaten on Earth. Darkness is a fecund presence to be deeply interacted with. Birds sing different songs at night, the Earth has a different hum, and our bodies are different in the darkness. Our perception is different. Lilith lives in and draws her power from this darkness.

Spirituality is not only believing in *spirit*, but *experiencing spirit*— that which has no physical form but is everywhere present in what is categorically called the *darkness*. Because Western minds cannot believe in anything other than that which they can see, what is black—darkness, the unseen—has become the thing that most frightens us. We deny ourselves this experience.

Ritual
Eating the Darkness

Darkness is not something to be feared. It is your friend. Take the time to be with the darkness. Go for a walk when it is dark outside. Can you feel the plants and trees continuing to grow even in the absence of sunlight?

Make time to sit outside when it is dark. Do you understand the darkness is feeding you? Feel all the ways darkness nurtures you. Feel how the darkness pushes against and penetrates your skin, entering your inner darkness.

As you sit in this darkness, imagine yourself growing roots like a plant, pulling all the rich nutrients and minerals of the inner Earth up into your body. Wash your endocrine system with this dark liquid. Let your pineal gland have a bath. Imagine it thick as molasses, pouring over and through these deep inner glands, being washed in this rich, earthen darkness. Breathe this in fully. Go to sleep nourished in this darkness. Deeply rest. Deeply rest. Deeply rest.

Chapter Seven

Lilith is the Shadow Woman

Robert Johnson states in *Owning Your Own Shadow* that some of the pure gold of our personality is relegated to the shadow because it can find no place in that great leveling process that is culture.[11] For women, this seems to be especially true.

The definition of what is viewed as acceptable female behavior is so restrictive—the boxes we force ourselves into so tiny—that we must send most of ourselves away. Because use of the more "powerful" parts of our personalities may feel dangerous or threatening, women will, quite often, hide them within the protective shelter of their shadows. Unfortunately, these can include her strength, her intellect, her wisdom, and her intuition.

Because we women feel inclined to keep ourselves "small," we carry large shadows. Because we are afraid to own the contents of our shadows, we cannot become whole. Because we do not own them, they possess us.

What we fear, and therefore deny or repress, becomes our shadow. One of the largest misconceptions still pervading the Western world is that our shadows possess only "negative" things; that the shadow is necessarily evil.

The shadow, so often perceived as evil, demonic, or frightening, is, in fact, merely an absence of light. What we refer to as our *dark side* is only that which we do not let others see; what we do not wish to acknowledge about ourselves.

Our shadows—those disowned parts of ourselves that fill the air surrounding us—are comprised merely of the things we perceive to be or have been (both directly and indirectly) taught are unacceptable, threatening. That does not mean they are necessarily bad; they could just as easily be positive things. Quite often, the most vital, interesting, the very essence of a person is banished to her darkness.

Energy will…*must*…move. What is pushed down and rejected—denied—will go somewhere. "Unless we do conscious work on it, the shadow is almost always projected; that is, it is neatly laid on someone or something else so we do not have to take responsibility for it." [12]

Since shadows are the driving force behind projections—the things which allow us to place blame, and thereby not take responsibility or be moved to action—they are the perfect tool for any oppressor.

A woman who is afraid of her own power will hate a powerful woman. A woman who has pushed down her intellect will be jealous of a woman who displays hers. To keep our own power dead, we need to kill the power in each other. This takes up our time, uses all our energy—keeps us eternally busy.

A common theme in what remains of the myths and stories of the Goddess is that of a female character making a descent into the underworld. There she meets a "dark sister" whom she must assimilate. Indeed, many feminist scholars have suggested that the "female quest" is an inward journey—a trip through the labyrinthine course of the soul.

Psychological health is only possible through the integration of the many parts of the self. It is in the journey through her own "underworld" that a woman meets her unaccepted selves and begins to integrate them.

Ritual
Ritual of the Golden Shadow

How about letting yourself be smart? How about letting yourself have a voice? How about believing in yourself? How about owning your own misery and your own jealousy and your own small self when it shows up? How about letting yourself be whole? How about letting yourself be *golden?*

Who is locked up in your shadow? You can easily find out by looking at what you don't like in other women who "push your buttons." Make a list of those buttons. If you want to be creative, you can draw them as buttons and color them, cut them out, and hang them up. However you want to interact with your own buttons is your choice. These are your buttons, no one else's. What are those buttons telling you about you?

Slowly, by owning them as your own, you will remove the buttons one by one. Soon, there are none left to push. New ones will surely appear. Notice them and look at them. What do they want? What are they trying to tell you about you? This is your shadow material.

Your shadow is a rich garden of information for you. Let it shine. Polish it golden. Let it be reflective rather than absorbent. Let it come out and play.

Chapter Eight

Lilith is a Woman Who Exposes the Truth

Women's lives for thousands of years have been supported by a basic denial of themselves and the truth of their experience. We have inherited generation upon generation of cover-ups and lies: lies about what really happened and lies about women's experiences of it. Because of this, women have become the most notorious of liars.

I'm sure every woman can fill pages with lists of these lies. Here are but a few: "I'm O.K." "I'm not angry." "There *is* such a thing as domestic bliss." "I don't have any needs, wants, or desires of my own." "I am happy to stand in the background of other's lives and simply serve."

I have observed that the person a woman most fears to offend is her mother. Common rhetoric goes something like this: Mothers have not been able to support their daughters, both literally and metaphorically, in their search toward selfhood. The daughter's search uncovers the mother's lies.

We women have been told...*taught*...to lie. We have been instructed to lie for the sake of protecting our vulnerable mothers whose reality, indeed sanity (we have been told), rests so precariously upon fabrication and repeated denial of self. We have perceived our own development as threatening. We have been told the person it most threatens is our mother.

In her book *The Hungry Self*, Kim Chernin discusses this dilemma. She has observed women developing eating disorders when they are about to surpass their mothers' lives. They literally stop their physical and, in turn, psychic development through becoming completely immersed in the obsessiveness of an eating disorder. This form of "self-sabotage" spares the mother the painful exposure their own development might cause. These women, Chernin says, "establish a predisposition to guilt about one's own growth and development, which is seen against a background of another's diminishment and depletion." [13]

This disorder need not only apply to the extremes of anorexia and bulimia, but also to the simple chronic overeating and undereating, or the preoccupation with food intake more commonly referred to as "diet." I have not yet met a woman for whom this relationship is "clean." If this can, in fact, be viewed as symptomatic of our relationships to our mothers (mother, mother in us, divine Mother), possibly we could begin to do something about it.

In *Thoughts Without A Thinker*, Mark Epstein discusses the differences between the Eastern and Western perceptions of Mother.

Epstein writes about the Tibetan Buddhists' use of guided meditation "to cultivate compassion and tranquility of mind." One of the commonly used meditations involves "recognizing all beings as our mothers ... the psychic root of this practice is the unambivalent love that the Tibetan population is able to summon for their own mothers." However, Epstein goes on to note, "Westerners have a difficult time with this practice: their relationships with their own mothers are much too conflicted." [14]

So, what is it that has happened in the West to cause us to feel so "conflicted" about our mothers? When we consider the fact that all women—whether they give physical birth to a child, adopt or remain childless—will, at some point in their lives, play the role of mother, why would we allow this situation to persist?

If we daughters, who all have mothers who had mothers, will go on to be mothers, often to daughters—why is it that we allow all of these relationships to remain conflicted, strained, polluted?

Is it not an underestimation of our own mothers to believe that they cannot handle the truth? Yes, the truth of our experiences is most often painful, horrifying. If we finally admit to the truth of our experience, it means also facing the truth of our participation in its enactment. But who is to say that this is a good reason to not "become" the women we "know" ourselves to be? Who is to say that sparing one kind of pain is worth experiencing another? Who was it that first decided mothers are unable to handle the truth? How degrading! How condescending!

"Surely it is time," Chernin argues, "to free both mother and child from the need to hide the raw anguish by which our mothers have lived. For it is the hiding and disguising, rather than the anguish itself, that is causing trouble for both mothers and daughters of this generation, whether we see ourselves as the mother or her child." [15]

Do we wish for our own daughters to view us in such a tiny, cramped way? Do we want our daughters, when they assume the role as Mother, to be thought of as a person too constrained and limited to deal with her own reality? If we begin to stretch our minds back through all the mothers before us and forward to all the mothers yet to come, we begin to see how truly urgent this issue is. Can we start to see our mothers as strong, validating women—the women who mothered us? Can we indeed offer this to our daughters?

The Original Lie
What is the cause of all this lying, anyway? All this lying springs from the original lie—the lie that cuts women into two, the lie that Eve was the first female. The lie that Lilith never existed.

Lilith, being ominously referred to as "Adam's first wife," disproves this. The truth is, our original parents lied to us. All these years we have been living according to this lie. This "truth" can cause tectonic plate movements inside the psyche of a woman. As well it should, because these seismic movements create the space needed for the whole truth. The whole truth is, Lilith is not just "Adam's first wife" (that is only what she has been reduced to), she is but a mere representation of what existed, the kind of woman that inhabited the Earth—and hints at a civilization in which she was welcome—for well over 30,000 years before Eve.

For well over 30,000 years before Eve, whole women like Lilith were the norm. Their strength and confidence were gleaned, in part, from the most basic understanding that all life comes from the female; that it is the female who possesses the power to create, regenerate, and reproduce life. In these cultures, no trace of violence remains. There is no hierarchical stratification. Men and women lived in community together, co-creating their reality, their lives, their love.

The original lie that we continue to be taught, the biggest lie of all—whose support requires a woman to cut her psyche into two—is that the first humans, in fact the Earth and all the universe, were created by a man.

If there is anyone who has ever seen a man give birth, let them step forward now. Otherwise, we reach the inevitable conclusion that we women have been supporting, protecting, and promoting the most fundamental, the most bogus, of lies.

Who indeed are women protecting? For whom are we really lying? Surely our mothers—most of whom labored to deliver us, assisted another woman in birth, or whose body ovulated and bled almost every month of her adult life—are well aware from whose body comes life.

Ritual
Unraveling Core Beliefs

Maybe you don't care that Adam had a first wife. Maybe you don't believe in God giving birth, so the lie about Lilith does not have an impact on your life. It is still possible there is some other fundamental lie or mistaken belief that has been running your life or actions in some way that needs uncovering and that you need to free yourself from. It doesn't matter which truth needs to be exposed. It is just that Lilith exposes truths. We all have our own truths and our own lies.

What is your fundamental lie? Take some time to really think about it. Is there a fundamental lie upholding all or any of your beliefs?

Are you able to ask yourself regularly, "Do I believe that?" "Is that really my truth?" Do you know what your truth is at any given time?

Is there a part of yourself that wants to exist that you have been told does not or cannot because of a fundamental lie? Why are you supporting this lie? Can you stop lying? Or does it feel too devastating?

To trace the path of a lie, it is helpful to follow a thought or feeling that is troublesome. These are often found in places that are repeatedly difficult for us—relationships, money, inner emotional turmoil, and stress. Feel into one of these thoughts and try to trace it backwards. Call in Lilith to help you with this.

I feel _____ because I believe _____.
I believe _____ because I was taught _____.
I believe _____ because everyone else _____.
I believe _____ because this is just the way it is.

Gauge the truth of each of the statements you have written in your body. Notice if your body feels a certain way when something is not its truth. When a statement does not feel true in your body, trace it back further using the previous technique once again. Where did the belief originate? What kinds of actions has it caused you to take? It can be difficult to do this kind of unraveling because sometimes we can find at age 60 we have been operating out of a mistaken belief about something our whole lives. But it is important work to do and leads to ultimate freedom.

Chapter Nine

Lilith is the Savior of Stillborns

Except as a demon, a witch, or a bitch, there is no place for a powerful woman in our society. A woman of power is the very thing men are taught to hate and women are taught to fear. A woman who uses her power risks banishment, isolation, physical abuse, and even murder. It is an entirely normal, and what could be called "healthy" reaction, that for protective purposes women would begin to hide or repress their power.

The most horrible, mean-spirited lie to be spread about Lilith is that she is a child killer, a murderer of babies. Could there be a worse thing to be?

The reason for the inception of this particular rumor was the recognition of Lilith's presence in the nursery at the time of the birth of a child, most especially when the child was stillborn.

Because Lilith was seen in the nursery at the time of the loss of a child, she was accused of murder. In fact, she was there because the mother, seeing that her child was in distress, had summoned her. Once, it was well known that Lilith would take care of the soul of the child who was born without the life force because Lilith is the Savior of Stillborns.

Ean Begg, a scholar of Black Madonnas, sees Lilith as but another manifestation of the Black Virgin, and tells us that "it is characteristic of Black Virgins that they resuscitate dead babies long enough to receive baptism and escape limbo." [16]

In Gnosticism, Lilith is "a spirit who is friendly and helpful toward the pregnant woman, responsible for the child's well-being before and after its birth." [17]

Lilith is referred to over and over again in introductions and personal stories of women everywhere—artists, writers, scholars—as the one who appeared to them at the moment of their spiritual awakening and birth to their creativity. They describe themselves as being led—guided by her on their journey. All seem to agree that Lilith is a force for women now. She comes at the perilous moment of our death and rebirth, the time when the life force hangs in the balance on this planet. She is here to resuscitate us. She has come to rescue our souls.

A person without power is stillborn. True power is inner power, the Goddess within, the life force.

Below the word "stillborn" in the Webster's New World Dictionary is the word "still life." Still life: *small, inanimate object.*

Could there be any better way to describe the ideal woman of the Western world? Is there a more perfect way to describe something that is powerless? For a woman to be anything more than a *small, inanimate object* is to pose a threat. Still life paintings are not passionate and moving, they are decorative and aesthetically pleasing.

Modern women, afraid of our power, afraid of the consequences the invocation of our power may provoke, decline Lilith's invitation, ignore the desire we feel deep within us, remain stillborn in our still lives.

Lilith is a mother. She has many children. They are called "Lilim." Her punishment for disobeying the father God is that she loses one hundred of her children each day.

Lilith is the first woman. Lilith is our mother. These children are us: women. We are all her daughters. Let us finally end Lilith's punishment. Let us find a way to live.

Ritual
Breathing Life to the Lifeless

What is there within you that is yearning to be born? What within you has a "still" life? These parts of you are often what come to life and show themselves as envy or jealousy of other. Jealousy is a gift. It shows us what we want that we have not allowed ourselves to have. It has nothing to do with other.

What do you keep killing in yourself through behaviors of self-sabotage and self-doubt because it feels too scary to let it live?

At night, light a candle to Lilith, preferably a black candle. See and feel this unborn part. At first you may not be able to recognize it, or identify its form. Allow it to slowly reveal itself to you.

Call Lilith to you. See her fly in and hover over this part of you. Allow her to breathe life into it. See her resuscitating it. Can you allow it? Make offerings of food and spirits to the Savior Goddess. Keep the candle burning. Do this as many times as you need to.

Chapter Ten

Lilith is a Sexual Woman

Lilith is sexual. Of all the writings about her, the ones pertaining to her *unbridled promiscuity* emit a certain terror. Her sexuality—controlled and enjoyed by her—evokes in the authors the greatest fear.

Indeed, the main reason for Lilith's banishment and subsequent punishment is due to her refusal to submit to Adam sexually. Their fight starts because Lilith, quite frankly, wants to be on top. Adam complains to God because Lilith refuses to lie beneath him during intercourse. This may seem a petty, unimportant squabble, but that is only because we still do not understand, we women have not yet recognized the fact that we no longer own our sexuality. In this very fight is where we lost it.

Sexuality is power. Spirituality is sexual. Power is spiritual. Sexuality is spiritual power. When we open our bodies to receive Her, our hips widening to Her entering us, Her energy surging in waves through us, we are having a sexual, spiritual, and powerful experience all at the same time. Separating these three—sex, spirituality, power—leads to the disaster we are currently living.

True mystical experience is orgasmic. True orgasm is mystical. The ultimate experience of the two is the same. There is no difference in the outcome. Differentiation lies only in the way used toward access.

What is sexuality? Our sexuality has nothing to do with another person, another person's body, another person's desires. We can have a shared sexual experience with another person, but it is not necessary for another person to be present in order for us to experience our sexuality.

Our sexuality is just that: ours. It is our own. Our sexuality is the way in which we experience our environment—the heightened sense of awareness that stems from opening to the sensual experience. We have been given so many ways to experience the sensual world around us, our senses each possessing their own unique signature. To smell, to feel, to taste, to touch, to see—so many ways to consume beauty.

Through a sexual encounter with another we may express and share the energy moving around, through, and between us. These feelings we name "love," "passion," "lust." The same energetic encounter is described with deities/entities of every spiritual tradition.

The term applied then is "divine love," but it is merely a

different term used to describe the same energy—the energy that permeates the universe always, which we are able to tap into and channel through our physical bodies.

Our sexuality is sacred because it channels cosmic energy through our bodies. Spirituality and creativity do the same thing. Our sexuality is a personal possession which, when shared, becomes a gift.

We would never assume that a person could own, possess, or fight over another person's soul, but we believe, without hesitation, that one person can possess another's genitals—one of the main access points to the soul.

On the deepest level, this is where we—women—have allowed the current paradigm to infiltrate us. In the most violent ways, this is where it has penetrated us. More than anywhere, it has attacked us in our wombs; stolen our power over giving birth, buried our knowledge of how to control our fertility. We are threatened with the fear of unwanted, forced intercourse, keeping us out of the dark outdoors—our power time. Our vulvas have been cut into and torn apart, our breasts slashed off. We have pretended not to notice.

The most violent, emotionally charged, political debate in the United States—the most bloody war being waged in this country—is over women's reproductive rights. The source of this battle is based on the fundamental unanswered question over who owns a woman's womb. Do we really not know the answer to this question?

Of course, Lilith is sexual. She is a woman. She is a woman of ancient descent. She is a woman who is aware of her foremothers. She is a survivor—a survivor of the first 30,000 years. She remembers.

She remembers a time when a woman saw her own sexuality

mirrored in the physical world around her; when a woman understood her body in the seasonal swelling of the land in spring, the Earth oozing moisture; in the opening, the spreading apart of dirt in which to plant a seed, an opening from which later would emerge life; in the ripening fruit, the rounded mounds of mountains. Everywhere, she saw herself.

In the waning and waxing moon, she recognized her own cyclical menses. She knew on the deepest, most profound level that she belonged to the Earth as well as the sky; that she was a part of both and they were both a part of her. From this she acquired her power.

Daughters of Lilith, remember true power is derived from embodied sexuality.

Ritual
Offering Our Pleasure Back to the Earth and Sky

Earth my body
Water my blood
Air my breath
Fire my spirit

Where do her mountains live in your body? The rushing waterfalls, the running waters, the sacred pools and lakes; where do you find them within you? What is your grass? The telluric realm is under your skin. Can you feel it? Inside your body are her organs. Like you, she too has chakras.

Everything you do in your body affects Gaia's body. Her body affects your body. You are rooted to her. You live inside her reality. This is true sensuality and sexuality—understanding and experiencing your oneness with Earth, knowing deeply that your biology is her biology.

Feeding your embodied experience of orgasmic pleasure back to her is a great gift and valuable practice.

Make an offering of the fleshy pleasure of biological life and sex. Begin to offer her your pleasure when you experience it. When you feel sexual or sensual pleasure, no matter to what degree—extreme orgasm or the sensual scent of flowers flowing by on a soft breeze—take that moment in and then offer it back to her—the Earth, the cosmos, the Goddess, the entire web of interconnectedness—through your heart space. You can do this on your own or ask a love partner or friend to do it with you after you have created that experience of pleasure together. Make these sensations prayer and offerings. Make a gift of embodied pleasure to the Earth.

Chapter Eleven

Lilith is a Bird Goddess

The Winged Goddess of Creation

Once, there was a dark, winged Goddess who came when people needed Her. She could take all their pain into Her being. She could absorb difficulty and trouble and transform it into something other— something useful. When one called out in hurt, it was the winged Goddess who hearkened, wrapping the sufferer in Her warm, sheltering feathers, embracing the anger, containing the rage.

If one howled with the agony of despair, others knew Lilith was with her. They awaited patiently the return of their friend from the time of suffering.

Excerpt from *Stories They Told Me*
by Theresa C. Dintino

Ritual
Being Held by the Bird Goddess

Take some time now to sit quietly and imagine a dark, winged woman, a Goddess, her cloak of feathers encompassing you, nurturing you; her sharp claws, talons, protecting you. Imagine knowing this presence, being sure it is there for you, knowing always you may go to her and she will take your pain, she will hold it for you, help you transform it into something new, something useful. This is the Bird Goddess, the twice-born redeemer, born of ashes, the Dark Goddess. She fears nothing. Nothing you can say to her will turn her away. Nothing is too shocking. She can hold it all.

Take some time to feel the energy of the Bird Goddess, to come into relationship with her. If we all had an embodied experience with her, we would live in a different world.

Above all, Lilith is a bird, a predatory bird of the night, a dark, winged woman—an owl. She soars through the air. She has the vision and precision of an owl, possessing all knowledge and understanding. She is also capable of great violence. But she uses her power only with the deepest integrity. She flies a silent and effective flight; a calculated, planned, and efficient journey.

That is true magic: To be all-knowing, all-powerful, and yet act with great restraint.

Once we welcome her back and open ourselves to her, Lilith will offer us this teaching.

Chapter Twelve

Lilith is a Strega

In his book *Lilith, The First Eve*, Siegmund Hurwitz traces the linguistic connection between Lilith, the owl, and the words "striga," "strix," and "stringes." "Strix" is literally the word for a screech owl. Ancient and classical cultures believed the strix, stringes, and striga to be demonic beings associated with owls. They "fly at night in the guise of birds to the cradles of children and suck their blood."[18]

"In all languages, so to speak, the word means a witch on the one hand and a predatory night owl on the other." In Italian, the word becomes "Strega." Hurwitz states, "In Italian, the word Strega means something akin to an evil old woman or witch, who is in league with the devil."[19]

Sounds like how Lilith is typically described.

After I wrote my two Crete novels, I decided to pursue a family legend I had been told about since my days as a child—that my Italian great-grandmother was a Strega. A Strega, in fact, is not an "evil old woman" or a woman in line with dark forces, the same as Lilith is not a child killer or a demon. A Strega is a medicine woman. My great-grandmother was a medicine woman in the Italian tradition.

This lineage was lost to my family. I had a few small fragments and memories to go on. *She was a midwife, a healer, a doctor, an herbalist. She knew how to cure the evil eye. It was difficult for her when she moved here because all the plants were different.*

To find out more, I decided to write a book about her. My novel, *The Strega and the Dreamer*, is the result of that effort. In doing the research, I connected to my great-grandmother and restored the lineage to my family. I am now a Strega, just like Lilith and my great-grandmother.

It is clear to me now that Lilith came to lead me on a journey to become a medicine woman in the tradition of my own lineage. It is beautifully eloquent. I am so glad I did not send her away.

What might Lilith want to lead you back to?

I encourage you to trust her and take the journey.

Blessed Be.

About the Author

Theresa C. Dintino is an ancestral Strega (Italian wise woman), earth worker, and initiated diviner. For more than 20 years Theresa has studied and practiced an earth-based spirituality. In 2011, she was initiated as a diviner in a West African tradition. She currently helps others reclaim their personal lineages through her divination work.

Theresa is the author of three novels: *The Strega and the Dreamer*, a work of historical fiction based on the true story of her great-grandparents; and *Ode to Minoa* and *Stories They Told Me*, two novels exploring the life of a Snake Priestess in Bronze Age Crete.

For more on Theresa or her work, visit:
http://www.thestregaandthedreamer.com and
http://www.ritualgoddess.com

Also by Theresa C. Dintino

The
Strega
and the
Dreamer

Theresa C. Dintino

The Strega and the Dreamer

The Strega and the Dreamer is the tale of Italian immigrants coming to America from the Abruzzi region of Italy at the turn of the last century.

Eva is an Italian Strega, a midwife and healer, fully committed to her small hilltop village. Marcello is a man with a dream of America— a dream that Eva does not share. Famine comes to the Abruzzi and Marcello goes to America, leaving his family behind as he searches for a more prosperous life.

Eva dedicates herself to her Strega duties and the people of the village. Though it is taboo for a woman to do so, with the help of a doctor from the city she secretly learns of modern medicine. When Marcello finally calls for her, Eva has a decision to make. She must choose between staying in her beloved Abruzzi where she has her family and her Strega calling, or moving to America, where midwifery is considered barbaric and is being systematically eliminated.

Ode to Minoa

When Aureillia, the young Snake Priestess in Bronze Age Crete, begins having visions of an unspeakable evil, her simple life is thrown into turmoil.

As a member of a Goddess-worshiping culture, her life is ruled by the cycles of the moon and a deep connection to the Earth, but soon will be affected by a far greater force. Visions of the future lead Aureillia to a loss of innocence and the discovery of her extraordinary power and the power in every woman.

Stories They Told Me

In an underground temple on the island of Malta, Danelle and Aureillia witness a vision of the future that shocks and horrifies them. Danelle journeys to Africa.

There, with the local shaman walking in and out of his own simultaneous lives, he explores the heartbreaking questions of his soul. Aureillia returns to her home in Bronze Age Crete, where shockwaves of a prophecy she told as a Snake Priestess years before resonate in ways unexpected. Can they find a way to change the future separation of men and women that appears to loom inevitable?

Endnotes

[1] Barbara Koltuv, *The Book of Lilith*, (Maine: Nicholas-Hays, 1991) pp.46-47

[2] Marija Gimbutas, *The Language of the Goddess*, (San Francisco: Harper & Row, 1986) p. 43

[3] Barbara G. Walker, *The Women's Encyclopedia of Myths and Secrets*, (New York: HarperCollins, 1983) p. 543

[4] Ibid., p. 542

[5] Alice Miller, *Thou Shalt Not Be Aware*, (New York: Farrar Straus Giroux, 1998) p. 6

[6] Siegmund Hurwitz, *Lilith–The First Eve*(Zurich: Daimon Verlag, 1992) pp.163-177

[7] Mary Daly, *Pure Lust: Elemental Feminist Philosophy*(HarperSan Francisco, 1984) p.291

[8] Theresa C. Dintino, *Ode To Minoa*, (Philadelphia: Sterling House Publisher, 1999). The Dance of Release is described in the novel.

[9] Theresa C. Dintino, *Stories They Told Me*, (San Jose: iUniverse, 2003). The Serpent of Fire is explored in this novel.

[10] Ted Andrews, *Animal Speak: The Spiritual and Magical Powers of Creatures Great & Small* (St. Paul: Llwellyn Publications, 1994) p.130

[11] Robert A. Johnson, *Owning Your Own Shadow: Understanding the Dark Side of the Psyche*(HarperSan Francisco, 1991) p.7

[12] Ibid., p.131

[13] Kim Chernin, *The Hungry Self: Women, Eating & Identity*. (New York: Harper & Row, 1986) p. 122

[14] Mark Epstein, *Thoughts Without a Thinker: Psychotherapy from a Buddhist Perspective.* (New York: Basic Books, 1995) p. 175

[15] Chernin. p. 74

[16] Ean Begg, *The Cult of the Black Virgin*, (England: Arkana, 1985) p. 37

[17] Ibid., p.39

[18] Hurwitz, *Lilith—The First Eve*, p.45

[19] Ibid., p.46

Made in the USA
Coppell, TX
10 May 2023

16654169R00039